Children's Creative Play

Other books by Karin Neuschütz

Sewing Dolls

Creative Wool:
Making Woollen Crafts with Children

Making Soft Toys

Children's Creative Play

How Simple Dolls and Toys Help Your Child Develop

Karin Neuschütz

Floris Books

Translation: Polly Lawson
Photographs: Thomas Wingstedt
Drawings: Karin Neuschütz

First published in Swedish under the title *Lek med mjuka dockor* by
Bokförlaget Robert Larson AB, Täby
First published in English in 1982 by Larson Publications Inc, Burdett, NY
First published in Great Britain in 1985 by Floris Books
This second edition published in 2013

e   This book is also
     available as an eBook

MIX
Paper from
responsible sources
FSC
www.fsc.org   FSC® C013056

British Library CIP data available
ISBN 978-086315-964-0
Printed in Great Britain
by TJ International Ltd, Cornwall

Contents

Introduction

One beautiful summer day, my children were playing. Then playing turned into fighting over their things, so we went on a trip to find raspberries instead. We left all their toys behind, took a pail, and set out.

When we reached the raspberry patch, they became content. They stuffed themselves full of berries, and began to play together again.

My oldest child found an old dry tree branch in a ditch. 'Look, a factory! Come and see all the pipes. What's inside them?'

'Raspberry juice of course!' said my younger child.

Then they got stones to use as trucks and they transported the raspberries, which they crushed and pretended to pour into the twigs on the tree branch. Other little sticks became workers, rushing here and there. They laughed and showed me their remarkable factory, as proud as if they'd invented something revolutionary.

In fact, that was exactly what they'd done.

Their raspberry factory had been created out of virtually nothing. As children have done throughout history, they had made very simple little models of people. Little pieces of wood or stone become alive and walk around – the simplest of dolls.

Children often have such strong imaginations and ability to play that they prefer simple, natural things to fancy toys. They pretend to be the mother of a pillow wrapped in a scarf; they tie string around crinkled-up newspaper and drag it around like a dog. Parents who have invested a lot in their children's toys can feel somewhat disillusioned. My children once adopted a piece of wood, named it Harvey and lovingly tucked it into a pram. The cloth doll I'd sewn for them was mercilessly dumped out of the pram, onto the floor. Harvey got all the attention.

Parents need to remember that children don't play to make their parents happy. They don't play with toys they've been given to show their gratitude; they play because they *have* to play, because they're built to. Play is one of the main ways that children grow and develop. Play prepares children for adult life. They get little tasters of the adult world: pretending to be a mother or father; travelling, shopping, building a factory.

So as a parent, I know I mustn't feel hurt when my cloth doll lies forgotten on the floor, while wooden Harvey is dressed up in the doll's sweater. Instead, I should feel happy that their imagination is powerful enough to resist my influence.

One day, after a while, Harvey was thrown into the fireplace. My daughter saw me putting other pieces of wood on the fire, and in that moment, Harvey became a regular piece of wood as well. And in he went.

'Oh, Harvey burnt up,' she noted calmly. 'But he'll come back soon,' she comforted herself.

'I'm sure he will,' I said, mentally calculating that there are lots of pieces of wood or pillows that can become dolls. But my daughter looked around for her soft cloth doll; apparently, she now needed it again.

Why do children so often choose such strange objects to use in their play? Why don't they just take the beautiful, ready-made things that we give them? Perhaps simply because children yearn to use their own lively imagination. They want to create by themselves; they don't want to just 'consume'. If they have different materials available – paper, crayons, empty boxes, fabric, blankets, pieces of wood and leather, pillows – and if they can use some pieces of furniture as building material, they can always build a raspberry-juice factory. If they're given toys where characteristic gestures and features are only gently suggested, their own imaginations can add what is missing.

Ultimately, as we'll see in this book, nourishing children's imaginations during childhood can influence their lives as adults: both in how they accomplish tasks, and how they relate to their fellow human beings.

Living through play

As soon as children learn something new, they start to play with their new ability, practising and testing it. And as they develop, they tackle increasingly difficult tasks. Children who have just learned to walk start to take little dance steps; children who can talk start to sing and rattle off nonsense words; children who can dress themselves start to dress up or put clothes on backwards, just for fun.

A three-year-old girl who has recently understood that she is 'I' pretends she is someone else – a little squeaking mouse, or a baby. She is testing the limits of her own 'I' by changing roles.

As soon as children get used to their home and learn what rugs and furniture are for, they can't wait to transform them, recreating the everyday into an adventure: the rug becomes an island, the floor an ocean, the chair a rowboat. The curtains are drawn and day becomes night. The shades go up and it's morning already.

Children practise all skills through rhythmic repetition. It is through play that children enter into life. And all the time their eyes follow grown-ups in their activities – for one day they will also grow big.

The consciousness of five and six-year-old children expands to the point where they can appreciate the bigger picture. They are interested in *why* we do the things we do, and they become more purposeful in their own activity. Everything they encounter in life is worked through in play. Whole worlds appear: schools, hospitals, families, theatres. Children at this age start to imagine what adults do, what life is 'all about'.

Until the age of seven, children use a huge amount of energy just to control and come to terms with their bodies. Around seven this energy is then released, and can be used for imagination instead. Children's memories develop; they can think more rationally, and think about the future.

They are more aware of time. As they start school, they play games with rules and practise coordinating with other children.

Nine and ten-year-olds are collectors. They want to understand how the world is organised, so they construct machines, draw houses in cross-section, develop factories and communication systems. They develop their own interests, becoming specialists and collecting facts. As they start to feel more grown up, they criticise adults more readily, often showing less respect and getting into trouble. It's at this point that children effectively stop playing.

To summarise, the imagination-forces in young children are hard at work developing their physical bodies, growing and shaping the organism.

Their imagination is released as they turn six or seven and become more comfortable with their body. These forces can now be transformed into soul activities, creativity and sensitivity.

Out of this living imagination comes teenagers' mental abilities, their clarity of thought and powerful ideas.

That's a useful overview of how children play at different ages. But there are children who can't play, who don't want to or don't have the energy to play, or who just rush and run around without being happy with what they are doing. How can we help them?

I believe that we always have to start with ourselves when we are trying to discover the reasons for a child's disharmony. Our own state of being is the well from which children draw inspiration and joy of living. They hover near us in all that they do; they want to be like us in every way. To guide our children we must therefore start by attending to ourselves. If the people around a child are happy and active, the child is likely to be too.

Taking the time to slowly and peacefully make a doll for a child can be a nice way to get close to him or her. As I sit and sew, I think about the child whose doll this will be. The child certainly senses the love and care that I 'sew into' the doll.

In this book I describe my own experiences of how children play at different ages, of how they are affected by their surroundings and by the people around them. My views have slowly come through work with my own and others' children. I have learned a lot from my own childhood memories and through studies of child psychology and pedagogy – mainly works by Rudolf Steiner and many of his followers. I have picked up many things from today's Steiner-Waldorf schools, and have tried to synthesise it all into a uniform whole.

I remember Gisela Richert with gratitude; it was she who initiated me into the art of making soft dolls.

Finally, I want to emphasise that where Waldorf dolls are discussed in this book, they are regular wool or cloth dolls that have been made by hand in many parts of the world, in some cases for generations. Waldorf schools can't claim sole ownership of these dolls; they are, however, gladly used in Waldorf kindergartens, and I believe they're a wonderful addition to homes as well. For more detail on how to make some of these dolls, please see my other books in English: *Sewing Dolls*, *Making Soft Toys*, and *Creative Wool* (see Further Reading on page 118).

1. Dolls: Their History and Relevance Today

Soft dolls, whether rag dolls, knot dolls or Waldorf dolls, are a wonderful plaything for children. It's hard to trace their exact history: many ancient dolls made of wood and clay have been found in archaeological excavations dating back hundreds and even thousands of years. Before people had tools, children probably just played with stones or a piece of wood which were roughly the shape of a human being. Simple, improvised dolls would have been common, but they were also played with until they fell apart or were thrown away, so few survive. And when archaeologists find pieces of cloth and wood together, who can say categorically that they were originally an early soft doll?

The history of dolls is therefore mainly a chronicle of fancy and beautiful dolls made in more recent centuries. In the western world in the sixteenth, seventeenth and eighteenth centuries, dolls were usually made from wood, wax or papier-maché. There was often a layer of wax on the face, to give the doll a melancholy expression and shiny skin. (Beware taking these dolls too close to the hot stove!) Fancy dolls like these had their heyday in the 1800s, especially in France where major clothiers used dolls as models for their elegant wardrobes.

By the nineteenth century, many dolls, especially in France and Germany, were made from glazed porcelain ('china dolls') or unglazed bisque ('bisque dolls'). Their bodies were often made from cloth or leather, and were fashioned to represent adult proportions. Childlike dolls didn't appear until the latter half of the century.

The emergence of celluloid and plastic as materials in the early twentieth century changed doll manufacturing significantly. Now that dolls could be mass-produced, they became affordable enough that every home could have one. Previously, many poor families had only been able to buy a porcelain head, to which they sewed a body, and this fancy doll would often sit up on a high shelf in the parlour, perfect and untouchable, while the children played with homemade dolls. The fancy doll was admired by visitors, and only taken down on special occasions. Children might fantasise about being able to play with the beautiful, unreachable doll.

I wonder whether, in fact, children didn't secretly take down these fancy dolls when their parents weren't around? Children in all cultures probably quietly played with the little house-god, the fetish, the saint figure or sculpture when no one could see. They were all important adult 'dolls', and therefore represented a special power to children.

Then suddenly there were plastic dolls, and there were lots of them. Adults didn't value them in the same way, because they were so commonplace. If a doll broke, you bought a new one. They became everyday.

These new plastic and rubber dolls replaced both the fancy doll on the shelf, and the homemade rag dolls. Now adults didn't have to make dolls for their children anymore, just as soon they wouldn't have to sing songs for them (as records became more common) or tell them stories (the radio and the TV would take care of that).

But perhaps the tradition of making dolls at home has only temporarily ceased. As more adults feel the need to be creative and crafts become popular again, perhaps the skills and enjoyment of doll making will be revitalised.

When the group of people around the first Waldorf school in Stuttgart, Germany, were thinking about suitable toys for their kindergarten and homes, they drew on their own cultural traditions. Dress-up dolls were commonly made in rural homes throughout central Europe at the turn of the twentieth century, and they were adopted by the Steiner-Waldorf movement as how dolls should look.

Dress-up Waldorf dolls

It is particularly the head which gives Waldorf dolls their characteristic look. The bodies are often made in different ways. Children at the Waldorf School were taught how to make them in their sewing classes, and how to stuff them with wool. Children learnt then, and still do in similar schools around the world, what a wonderful thing it is to make an image of a human being.

Dolls as images of human beings

There are collectors throughout the world who fill their homes and museums with dolls of all shapes and sizes. These dolls sit in their glass cases and look sadly down at visitors; not even in secret do children come and play with them (although perhaps the collector might?). People who collect dolls are often people who didn't play with dolls as children; they hide their unfulfilled desire to play with dolls behind an acceptable mask of being a collector.

The doll is special among toys because it is the image of a human being. Dolls can help us find our own identity. We can reveal our innermost thoughts, sorrows and joys to a doll friend. With a doll's help, we can dream ourselves away from a hard reality, or get ready for new baby brother or sister.

The Latin word for doll is *pupa*, and from this also comes the English word 'pupa', used for butterflies and other insects undergoing transformation. What wonderful symbolism: life can emerge from a doll, in the same way it does for a butterfly. There are some children who can see the butterfly in *every* doll: they have great empathetic feelings for all animals and dolls, and nurture all of them. Other children decide on one special doll, and keep it as their beloved childhood toy.

It's important that parents treat dolls with the same respect with which they treat real people. Children hitting and punching dolls shouldn't be tolerated, because if dolls are images of human beings, it could imply that it's okay to hit real people too. Dolls and people alike need tender care.

Dolls faces are very important, and can have a significant impact on a child. In Swedish, the word for doll, *docka*, means wound-up yarn, and reflects the simplicity that a doll should have. The stereotyped smile which is painted onto many plastic dolls imposes itself on a child in an unhealthy way, generating an artificial mood. Keeping the doll soft and simple, on the other hand, with only dots for the eyes and mouth, allows the child freedom to 'fill in the gaps'. Such dolls can change their expression, in the eyes of the child, depending on the child's mood. The doll is shaped by the child's play, not the other way round. The doll could even change gender, which would hardly ever be possible with a plastic 'girl' doll.

Some children like their doll to have a nose, in which case an extra dot can be added. If a child wonders why their doll doesn't have any fingers, a few stitches to suggest them are all that is needed. Our soft doll also doesn't have any gimmicks like a monotonous voice mechanism which says, 'Mama, mama!' Such things often attract children's curiosity — what's that making that noise? — and frequently result in a child dismantling the dolls to explore the contents inside.

I clearly remember the strange, slightly aggressive feelings I had as a child because my rubber doll had a stopper on its rear. The stopper was so that doll could be emptied of bath water, but this didn't stop me feeling uncomfortable and angry about it — it was a defect that spoiled my doll. I couldn't forgive the manufacturer. I also

23

disliked the text imprinted on the doll's back – I can still feel how my own back itches there, sometimes.

Children are strongly influenced by their most loved toys. Therefore, as parents, carers and educators, we should ensure they are good, positive influences.

2. Babies

Environment and stimuli

For little newborn children, life appears dreamlike. They rest in our arms with total faith, receiving care and warmth, unable to protect themselves from anything.

Only when babies are feeling warm and well do they reach out with their eyes. They seem to wonder, where I am? They can lie quietly, and breathe in the room's atmosphere. Stimuli such as colours, lights, sounds, movements and smells nourish young babies as much as food. They absorb everything: they have no clear boundaries for what is inside and outside their own bodies. The state of being of the people around them – including their thoughts and feelings – penetrates and shapes the young infant.

Sudden noise or sudden cold frightens babies, making their blood vessels constrict. They must then use all their energy to raise their body temperature again, distracting them from the outside world until well-being is restored. All sudden or acute impressions on their senses are a setback in their attempts to explore the world. We should therefore protect young infants from overly strong sense impressions, for example, by surrounding their crib with pastel colours, and making sure the nursery is always peaceful.

Rhythm and repetition are also very important for babies. The fact that the same things are repeated every day, in a certain pattern, gives the baby space to start to recognise itself. Babies don't need any additional stimuli in the first few months: daily care, being with their mother and other key adults, the impressions from different rooms and occasional trips out are more than sufficient.

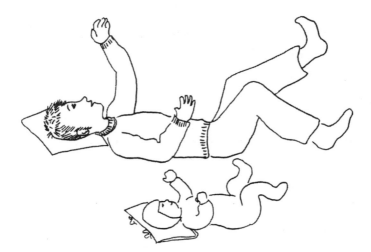

Understanding children, and putting ourselves in their place, are important steps to understanding their needs and being able to nurture them. In the case of a baby, try lying on your back on the floor, without being able to turn over onto your front. Wave your arms and legs around a little; turn your head from side to side. Try to imagine you don't know what anything is: try to see furniture, curtains and lamps only as shapes and spots of colour with depth. What an amazing place you can find yourself in! Sometimes, lights appear on the ceiling; othertimes, it's dark. But without using your adult intellect, you can let the sense impressions flow over you.

Types of stimuli

In many cultures, babies are carried around the home by their mother, as she carries out daily activities. If we don't want to, or can't, carry a baby in this way, a basket on wheels can be a good substitute. It can be a kind of day bed for a baby who starts to be increasingly awake during the day, and can lie there following our movements with its eyes.

It's important not to use a baby's sleeping place as a safe place to leave the baby during the day. Babies should get to know two different environments: a quiet sleeping place, and an active daytime place.

If a child is left alone in their sleeping crib during the day, they can come to associate the crib with loneliness and disappointment. Imagine yourself into the baby's situation: you have been put in your sleeping crib during an 'awake' part of the day. You can't move anything except your head and limbs. You can't talk. You desperately want to be close to a soft, warm, familiar person. You call out; someone comes, wonderful! But she assumes you're bored, and instead of taking you with her, she hangs a dangling mobile above your crib. A row of bright red, blue and yellow thing in front of you makes it hard to see her, or see the room.

You are disappointed: imagine instead if you could have lain in a basket on wheels in the same room as her, and seen what she did instead.

These kinds of so-called educational toys for babies are, in my opinion, totally unnecessary. Babies are naturally eager to explore their surroundings. They try hard to work out why their mother looks serious, why their crib is warm, and why their stomach aches.

Large mirrors, common in nursery schools, can throw young children out of their natural 'in-the-moment' state. Young children shouldn't be made aware of how they look, and it can be confusing: if I'm here, how can I also be there? Babies who have become used to mirrors can start making faces in them, becoming affected and self-conscious. They can look at themselves through others' eyes, losing their pureness and spontaneity.

For babies to find their own identities, they don't need mirrors, but rather other people. Makers of 'educational' baby toys try to persuade parents that children need these things to develop properly and 'get ahead'. In fact what babies need is simply to play with their fingers and toes, to try to turn around, to feel the sheet and blanket, pull at their sleeve, and wonder how their clothes sometimes change colour.

Above all, what babies need is the contact of loving adults. When their mother or father picks them up, life becomes rich. There's fuzzy hair to pull, a big nose to poke your finger into, a strange opening full of white shiny things that opens and closes, and makes strange, fun sounds. There are two round spots surrounded by tickly hairs, which also open and close. And there are flying fingers and hands

which can carry, stroke, tickle, clap, and form themselves into almost anything!

Additionally, these adults are always changing: buttons, ribbons, necklaces, bracelets, watches all vary. And sometimes another large person appears, with new facial features, smells and sounds.

Even when out for a walk, many people seem to feel that the baby might be bored. Instead of an enclosed, protective pram, they buy a panoramic, open one so the baby has a 'good view'. Or they hang up a string of brightly-coloured plastic across the baby's line of sight, obscuring clouds, houses, walls and trees.

The most important thing is that eye contact is maintained between adult and child, so that the mother's face can calm the child if something frightening happens. The best arrangement for small babies is to carry the child in a carrier on the adult's front. That way, the adult's voice can also be heard over outside noise.

One final word on outdoor walks: if possible, avoid using a dummy (pacifier). These can prevent the child getting involved in the sights and sounds of the walk; they often cause the child to turn in on itself, and become dreamy. If you use them, pacifiers are best saved for sleeping time.

Once babies can sit up, and start to crawl, they naturally want to explore, touch and taste (another form of touching) everything. Everyday objects such as wooden spoons, jars, boxes, crinkly uncoloured paper, balls and balls of wool are perfect for this age. We don't always need to find new things: a familiar object can appear in a new light if it's presented in another room. Or, replace the wooden spoon that the child has been playing with for a long time, with another one which is a bit different. The baby is usually fascinated that the spoon has 'changed'. But getting new objects all the time can become tiring for babies.

When babies start moving around, it's harder to direct their attention. There's always a tempting bit of wire, or a dangerous piece of furniture. But at this age babies are still easily distracted, so carry them into another room where there are some fun shoes with strings, or a box with wooden blocks.

Babies use all their senses to test these objects, exploring how they taste, sound, feel, and whether you can lift them or pull them.

Summary

Babies can't protect themselves from damaging stimuli. It is our task to make their environment calm and secure.

Babies don't need toys; they need human closeness and warmth. 'Educational' toys like mirrors only confuse babies. The best toys are their own bodies and adult hands, faces and clothes.

Crawling-age babies should be able to explore their home in freedom and security.

Recommendations for play and toys for babies

Sometimes we, or other adults, still like to give babies a little something. We could make:

A knot doll in a light colour, small enough for a baby to pick up. Knot dolls are very versatile and can be made of cotton, silk or textiles. Use a square of material and a little wool or cotton rags for the bound-off head, then tie the knot hands to create the basic shape.

A simple mobile to hang over a changing table. Use wooden skewers, thread and wads of pastel-coloured tissue paper. It will move gently in the draft, and slowly change colour and light. (Unlike the mobile described earlier, this mobile merges gently with the baby's waking environment and does not demand interaction.)

A crocheted rattle. Crochet around and around, making an oblong shape that widens to a ball at one end. Stuff it with wool or rags, and sew a little bell into the middle of the ball before stitching it all together at the top. Make sure the bell cannot come out (this would be a serious choking hazard for a small child).

A soft cloth ball. Cut out four ellipse-shaped pieces of felt. Sew the wrong sides together, leaving one side open. Turn inside-out and stuff with washed sheep's wool, a ball of yarn, or cotton rags. Sew up the last side. Make sure it's small enough for a baby to hold in one hand.

Knot doll

3. Age One to Two

Imitation

In everything they do, children are driven by a strong desire to be like the adults around them. We do it first, and children do it after. Children who don't have 'upright' people around them can't learn to stand up. We are happy; the child is content. We worry; the child becomes anxious. We feel joy in working; children are free to play.

It's a great responsibility that parents and carers have. We can subscribe to all kinds of theories about how children should be cared for and stimulated, but if we ourselves are stressed and nagging, our ideas are worthless. It is our own state of being that children absorb and imitate.

Once children learn to stand up and walk, their shoulders and arms are freed from the strenuous business of crawling. Their head is finally upright, and children now feel more like the upright, walking adults around them. Soon, they start to use their new ability to reach things which were previously unreachable.

Often, children can walk more easily when they are holding something in their hand. Just the feeling of 'holding on' helps them to balance. As they become more confident, they become playful and take little dance steps and jumps. They delight in being able to follow a parent from room to room.

A little girl, let's call her Emily, is about 18 months old. She has a big brother. When her big brother and her mother clean the house, Emily comes toddling after them, carrying all kinds of things. She moves things here and there, for reasons unknown to her mother and brother. Actually, she's doing what they're doing: carrying things, and putting them down again. She doesn't understand the purpose of moving these things; she's just copying their external gestures.

Emily sits with a book and 'reads' with little wrinkles on her forehead. Her eyes focus closely on the page, then after a quick look, she turns the page and stares at the next one. She likes turning the pages, and she's seen from her parents' faces that reading is a serious activity.

By her second birthday, Emily has learned a lot about things. She knows that the broom belongs in the corner, that the cup belongs in the kitchen, and that the wastebasket is usually under the table, and so on. Her parents praise her neatness, and her big brother, Tom, is surprised by how willing she is to bring him his things. But Emily is not neat. She just finds joy in the fact that certain objects belong in certain places: the confusion of such a multitude of things has started to clear into a recognisable pattern.

Now that Emily knows where things go, she can play with her new knowledge. She puts her toothbrush among the forks, her shoes in her bed, and her pants on her

head! She finds this hilarious, and doesn't understand why everyone isn't laughing as much as her.

Emily is based on my experience of my own daughter's development, but the stages are universal. So many interesting things happen in a home. The English word 'interest' comes from Latin *interesse*, meaning to be in-between. This is exactly where children want to be: sticking their heads up in between me and whatever I'm working on. Their favourite thing is to join in with my activities, getting a little bucket and rag to help wash the cabinets, or working their little piece of dough when I bake. It's not anywhere near as much fun to bake when I'm cleaning, or clean when I'm baking. No, if I'm doing dishes, my daughter wants to do dishes–preferably in the same basin as me! If I sew, she wants a piece of cloth with a thick needle.

One time, when my daughter was two and a half years old, she happened to see me using a red crayon to colour the cheeks of a cloth doll I was making. She disappeared into another room, and all was quiet. After a little while, I could hear a pitiful moaning sound. I went into her room, and oh! all the dolls had scarlet fever: they were bright red, with the darkest of red wax crayons all over their faces. Fortunately, wax crayons wear off textiles fairly quickly.

So, children do as adults do. The precision with which they can acquire a typical trait from a parent is uncanny. If I myself have a sagging posture, I can't complain about my child's poor posture. If I toss all the toys and dolls together in a jumble in a box when I clear up, I shouldn't be surprised if my child handles toys roughly. If I write in books or make them dog-eared, I can be sure that my child will too – and her version will be a little livelier. Our children do as we do, because they love us and want to be like us.

Another reason that little children don't like letting their loved ones out of their sight is because they're not sure whether or not they're really there, when they can't see them. (The same is true for inanimate objects.) That's why peek-a-boo is such a popular game: we hide ourselves for a moment, then appear again. The reunion is joyful. From this game, children learn that we do come back.

For the same reason, beware of playing hide-and-seek with little ones, which can be scary for them. Older children hide themselves so well, the younger ones get anxious that they're gone for good. Small children want the older child to be hiding in the same place each time, so they can decide for themselves how long the uncertainty should last. Instead of hide-and-seek, small children really want to play hide-and-find!

Drawing and painting

Anna has a crayon. She is one-and-a-half years old. She has noticed that something appears when you move the crayon over a surface. At this stage, she doesn't understand that you should only draw on paper; that we'll have to teach her.

For now, she has a sturdy crayon and a large sheet of paper. First, she lightly whips her hand around, and stares in surprise at the result. Then she becomes bolder and moves her hand in wide curves over the paper. She gets faster, becomes more intense and presses harder. Her hand moves in large figures of eight, crossing back and forth, layer upon layer. There are whirls that never end. Now Anna wants to draw as often as possible.

We can learn things from Anna's drawing. Firstly, let her have thick crayons, such as block crayons which don't break. Drawing with a lead pencil or ballpoint pen has nowhere near the same powerful effect.

Look at her scribbles: there are forms that resemble the way a child would run across the room – a dance across the paper instead of across the floor. They can also resemble whirls of water, planet orbits, wind or plant shapes. Perhaps children 'know' more about these things than we realise.

Watercolour paint isn't suitable until Anna can understand the sequence of dip in water, then dip into paint, then paint. This rarely comes before the age of three, and then initially only with one colour at a time. When the time comes, give her a large paintbrush, use real watercolour paints, and let her paint on moistened paper so that the paint flows and shines.

Painting with the fingers seems wrong to me. Colour is like pure light, ethereal and intangible. Light and colour please the eye; why confuse them with mud pies?

The colour of toys

It is a widely held belief that children love bold colours. Many children's playgrounds and daycare centres are covered with strong primary colours and patterns. It can be hard to find a calm spot.

Colour and light nourish our bodies: we are affected by them right down to our smallest cell. Spending a lot of time in artificial light, for example, can have a detrimental effect on us. We also use colour to express the moods of the soul, and we can feel different in a yellow room than in a red one. We often use colour to describe our feelings: 'she was in a black mood, he was green with envy,' and so on.

Our eyes' ability to discern colours is truly amazing. And like all abilities, it can be developed or dulled. It is better

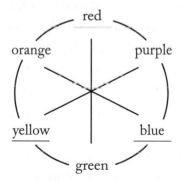

Colour wheel

training for the eye to interact with translucent, subtle colours than for it to meet solid, strong colours.

Let's spend a moment on how colours work. In the standard Goethean colour wheel are the three primary colours: red, blue and yellow. Opposite them are their 'complementary' colours: green, purple and orange. Mixing the primary colours gives us these secondary colours: yellow and blue give green, red and blue give purple, and red and yellow give orange. We get brown or grey when all three primary colours are mixed.

The whole spectrum of colours is present in normal daylight, and our eyes are very good at filling in the bits of the spectrum that are missing. For example, hold up a piece of solid blue paper against a white background, and stare intensely at the blue for a minute. Then move your eyes to the white next to it. You see an afterimage on the white: an orange spot.

This is because when you have looked at one of the colours, such as blue, your mind's eye generates the opposite colour, orange. For every colour we see, a complementary colour is generated within us.

Children can experience this phenomenon very vividly, and so the colours of their favourite toys and dolls are significant. When painting a child's room, try to use translucent colours which let the child experience the colour as light. The material underneath will shine through, and the colour won't feel constricting and lifeless. Small nuances are visible on the surface, which can stimulate a child's imagination.

Some toys can also be glazed, so that we can still experience some of the original material they were made from. Every type of wood has a unique structure, which is lost if we cover it with solid, plastic colour.

Materials: wool, wood and plastic

Jacob is two. He's about to go on a pretend trip, and he tests to see if he can lift all the things he wants to take. He puffs and feels strong when he manages to lift the big blocks, or Daddy's briefcase.

Jacob is learning to judge the weight of things from their volume, their shape, and the material they're made from. It's a learning process that will take many years. Even as an adult, Jacob will sometimes misjudge, or be fooled by a trick.

If we want to help Jacob learn, we shouldn't give him misleading information. But in fact, we do all the time. Look at that big plastic block – it looks much heavier than it is. Or his plastic doll – it's just an empty shell.

If a doll is both heavy and soft, and feels warm when you hold it in your arms, it makes it easier for a pretend mother or father to relate to it, to live in or through it. The child receives something back from the doll, and it's nice to cuddle in bed.

This can be achieved by stuffing dolls with sheep's wool. Wool fleece stores heat, and is not dangerous if the doll breaks. It's heavier than synthetic batting or rubber foam, and not as flammable. As a living, natural material, wool is also the best thing to use for a doll's skin, because it's soft and warm and resists dirt. Unfortunately, it's also expensive and often can't be found in 'skin' colours, so we frequently have to settle for cotton instead.

Wool and cotton fabric are such simple materials that children don't need to wonder about what's inside the doll and start taking it apart. It's lovely if a child can see a doll being made for them: not only do they develop a connection to the doll, but also to the doll-maker.

Variety

Children learn a lot through their fingers. They touch different surfaces and structures, and often like to have something soft in their hands when they are going to sleep. If their doll feels the same as their car, their boat and their blocks, children are robbed of a lot of experiences. Children who only have plastic toys live in an impoverished environment. Plastic also has no tone: unlike wood, glass or metal, it sounds totally dead when struck.

Wooden blocks are true to themselves. They are as heavy as they look, and they can be customised. A wooden car can be fixed and painted. A child can get to know it really well over many years. Wooden toys can be made in limited numbers, with great variation. Plastic toys, on the other hand, are mass-produced using expensive machinery.

Young children love simple shapes with endless variations, which are easy to grasp. Even the most blasé city child will collect pine cones, sticks, chestnuts, acorns and pebbles with touching devotion. Their concreteness is important: children can't experience a pine cone or a pebble in the same way by seeing one on television. They have to discover them for themselves.

If variety is important, what about a toy like Lego, where all the pieces are of a standard form? Lego doesn't have the living variety of horse chestnuts, but there are so many Lego variations now, surely it must be good for stimulating children's imagination?

It's true that Lego can inspire building projects. But the problem is that everything is built using Lego's own internal rules and conditions. Look at Jacob, now a little older, as he builds with Lego. He knows as soon as he feels the pieces snap together, they're held tight. So he builds quickly, carelessly in a sense. His hand repeats the same motion again and again. With the basic blocks, he doesn't have to consider whether this piece is able to attach to that piece – he is already 'locked in' to understanding how the pieces can be pressed together. And he knows one will fall off if he tries to put it on upside down, or on its side.

Now watch Jacob when he's building with irregular scraps from a carpentry shop. Every piece is different from the other. Before he even attempts to incorporate it, he weighs each piece in his hand, looks at it, and combines the information his hand and eye are giving him. He must subconsciously evaluate where he can put this piece, so it doesn't fall off. Then he has to place the piece carefully, with a light touch, and adjust it so it doesn't slide off.

It's clear that the irregular wooden pieces give Jacob a much richer experience than the Lego. They can also be reshaped, nailed together, painted – and if he gets tired of them, they can be burned up!

Lego requires less manual dexterity than the wooden pieces, and a more versatile imagination is needed to create something out of different pieces of wood. So if a child does nothing but construct with Lego pieces all day, it's worth asking whether there aren't other play materials which could add more variety, and allow more aspects of the child to develop.

The four elements

The four elements – air, fire, water and earth – are, along with the sun, moon, stars and the seasons, inexhaustible sources for activity in the preschool years.

We can blow light feathers and wads of cotton over the table. We can fly kites on windy days. We can fold paper swallows and make streamers that flutter or pinwheels that whirl, and we can chase snowflakes and wilted leaves that come floating down.

We can roast apples, potatoes and chestnuts. We can feed the fire with wood that we have sawn up and carried in; we fantasise about what is concealed in the embers. We find joy in the warmth and cook over the fire.

On the beach in the summer we can dig canals, fetch water in pails, or transform a sandbox into an island world. In spring creeks we can make waterwheels. And indoors we can play in the bathtub with mugs, funnels and gurgling water.

Children usually manage to find the last bit of unpaved piece of earth, wherever they live. And especially after rain it's wonderful to squish your feet into the mud. A garden is a wonderful place for digging and searching for worms and little crawling things.

It's exciting to dream up stories about the moon and stars, and to observe a real glowing sunset. There are also lots of songs and stories about the beings in the wind and the air, about the heat of the fire, about boats on the ocean, and about moles in the earth. (And if we don't know any, we can make them up!)

Try not to make nature too educational, thereby destroying children's spontaneous joy and immediate experiences of all that the natural world has to offer. Don't start explaining how rain is created and how snowflakes are made; don't destroy a child's wonder when a snowflake has become stuck on their coat and lies there gleaming white like a magic flower.

Let preschool children retain their wonderful images, for these images are real and true for them. In time, children get serious and want to learn how things 'really' are, but for now, give children images rather than numbers and science. If a child asks, 'How strong is the wind?' don't answer that it's blowing at forty miles an hour. Answer that the wind is so strong it can carry the leaves, and even knock mighty trees over sometimes.

Summary

Young children need to see adults who are
engaged in visible, practical jobs around them.

Very young children move around after
us, imitating our gestures, often without
understanding the purpose of our actions.

Scribbles are a child's movement, put down on
paper.

Colour is light, and light is nourishment for our
bodies. Treat colour with respect; paint in subtle
nuances to best develop the eyes.

Natural, simple, graspable materials are best for
preschool children. Give them variety, and give
them objects which are 'true' – a block that looks
heavy should also *be* heavy.

Give children toys they have seen being made, or
understand how they were made; or better yet,
that they helped to make.

Let the four elements, air, fire, water and earth, be
children's playmates.

Let children live with you, learning free from
educational instruction and explanations.

Recommendations for play and toys, ages 1–2

Knot doll (see page 3)

Large sack doll or cover-all doll

Doll's bed made of a cardboard box or wooden cradle, pillow, blanket and mattress

Doll's pram that can be pushed and won't easily tip over

Large soft ball to throw with both hands

Play blanket to hide under

Large basket or drawer to keep their things in

Irregular wooden blocks, scraps from a carpentry shop. (Older children can file off, sand, and paint them with watercolor and a fixing agent, or oil them with linseed oil and petroleum spirits, and give them to younger children as presents.)

Movable toy – for example, a wooden duck that waddles when pulled

Rocking horse

For outdoors: a bucket and spade, ball, and everything that nature offers!

Large sack doll

4. Age Three to Four

Rhymes and verses

Children eventually start to have more control over their bodily movements, and at the same time become more ambitious. They try to fly, and are surprised when they fall down. They do somersaults, try to stand on their heads, roll down grassy slopes, and twirl around on the swing.

In tandem with the pace of physical development, language also flourishes. The first laboriously expressed words were at the same time as the first tottering steps. Now that children can run and jump, they also start to rhyme, sing, and rattle off verses. Language is there to be explored! If you babble, sometimes you get real words, sometimes not. As they previously 'tasted' furniture, clothes and toys when they were crawling, children now 'taste' the sounds of their language. They practise everything from single sounds to intonation.

An adult's job is to provide lots of words, preferably funny ones which use lots of different sounds. Words are the cheapest toys we have at our disposal. However, don't be tempted to talk baby-language, just because it sounds cute. Children can feel offended if we use obviously 'baby-ish' words.

Rhymes and rhyming songs are perfect for this age. See a three-year-old's eyes shine as she rides your knees for 'Ride a Cock Horse to Banbury Cross'. Adults can often feel uncomfortable about the words of old nursery rhymes – they seem violent, or inappropriate – but children care more about the rhythm and rhyme than the content, and will quickly learn them by heart.

An otherwise difficult walk home from nursery can be improved with rhymes. Asking children about what they've done today forces them to think back, which can be tiring. Asking children to help plan dinner forces them to imagine the future, which can make their feet heavy. Making up rhymes about things they can see here and now, however, anchors them in the present, and helps their feet keep moving.

Dolls: just like me

At this age, children start to practice expressing feelings and experiences while playing with dolls. Children meet themselves in their doll, and give their doll life through their imagination.

Doll play starts early: even one-year-olds may bend down and kiss a doll. Two-year-olds will grasp a doll firmly, not caring if they pick it up by the head or the leg. When it's bedtime, the doll is pushed down into its bed and a blanket is forcefully pressed down around its sides. When it's time to get up, the blanket is swept off and the

doll pulled up, given a quick hug and dragged along on an expedition. It might end up in a puddle or the bath, in dirt in the yard, or stuffed under a piece of furniture. Sometimes it's realistically fed with yoghurt; other times, it's totally forgotten. Children of one and two often don't much care about dressing and undressing their doll: they just want a friend for special adventures. A doll with attached clothes – sometimes known as a 'cover-all doll' – is a good option for them.

Andy is four years old. He's been given a big dress-up doll with pyjamas just like his own. He looks lovingly at the doll, and tucks it in next to him every night. He has a friend; they're going to have lots of fun together.

When Andy gets older, he makes a parachute for the doll and drops it out of an upstairs window. When Andy starts to love cowboys and indians stories, the doll gets its own

Cover-all dolls with attached clothes

Mohawk costume. When Andy is sick, or when he goes travelling, the doll always comes too.

Andy has had a cold for a while, and he's tired of it. He regards his doll intently, suddenly lights up and say, 'Mum, my doll is so lucky because he doesn't have a nose. He can't get a cold!'

When children encounter rhymes and verses, this can transfer to their doll as well, and dolls can end up with interesting names: Curly-Burly, Workerman Doll, Mushi or Margerini. Sometimes, the doll is given the child's own name: then it really is 'just like me'.

Realistic toys

Andy may also want a soft toy. It's important to get him an animal that really looks like an animal – not an anthropomorphic version – but without being *too* detailed or realistic. The best animal toys are those which show a distinctive feature of the animal, for example, a wooden turtle which moves in a characteristic turtle way.

Caricatures aren't helpful. For a caricature to be funny, you have to already understand what the original looks like, but three and four-year-olds aren't at that stage. Look at their drawings of people: they don't contain much detail, especially of faces. They're not yet capable of critically observing what a face looks like – and we shouldn't teach them, because that consciousness belongs to a later age.

You sometimes come across puzzles for young children where a face is divided up into different pieces of the puzzle: a mouth on one piece, an eye on another. For children this is a completely alien way of dividing up a whole into abstract parts. It almost hurts them to cut up a face into different pieces, and it's unpleasant for them to remove part of a cat's ear, etc. in a large puzzle. A better option is a puzzle with sawed-out whole figures which can be played with when lifted out.

Other things to watch out for are puzzles or illustrations with thick black outlines. These lines don't exist in reality! It isn't helpful for children to think that two surfaces are demarcated by lines, when in fact they're just next to each other. My skin-coloured hand on the table isn't surrounded by a black line: it's skin-coloured, and it ends where the wood-brown table starts.

Drawing

The generous curves and spirals that filled Andy's drawings earlier have now focused into single crosses and circles. At three years old, Andy is struggling to draw a round ring. He holds his breath with the effort, and sighs with relief when he's done. The ring symbolises unity and wholeness: it is a closed room. Andy has started to experience the fact that there is an outside and an inside of him. He is the circle. He can now say 'I' with full consciousness. His earliest memories will come from this period.

In his drawing, the ring becomes a head. Arms and legs grow right out of the head. Might Andy's circle be different from Daddy's? Andy tests how his own ego relates to others' egos. He wants, and yet he doesn't want (what we

call 'obstinacy'). Andy needs to know where the limits are: we do this, and we don't do this. Then he feels secure.

Now four years old, Andy doesn't hesitate to start drawing: he just gets on with it. And something appears on the paper which gives him ideas for what to do next. As he draws, he describes what appears with amazement, as if someone else were drawing. 'It's a boat that's bobbing – and oh! it's so spotted! Does it have measles? And I see it's really windy because the flag is flapping. What's swimming under the boat? A dangerous fish!'

With delight, he shows Daddy what he's drawn. Later in the day, Daddy picks up the picture again, and Andy proudly tells him that it's a picture of a map, rain and cliffs. 'What?' Daddy says. He just manages to stop himself saying, 'This morning, you said it was a boat and a fish!' It simply isn't a boat any more for Andy; now he sees totally different things in the picture.

Change and transformation

Change and transformation are an inherent part of play at this age. Children don't need much to embark on free role play. Older ones will quickly give orders to younger ones: 'Let's say you're the mother and I'm the father, and you get to be the baby, and you can be the dog.' And they're off. If there aren't enough playmates around, dolls will do.

Now keep up: role changes, child birth and generation changes happen quickly in this age group. 'Now you're born, now you can crawl – no, let's say you can walk – now you're coming with me while I go shopping.'

The children look around the room and everything they see is usable. The sofa is a boat one moment, and the next moment it's a house with a blanket for a roof. At this age, children let impressions from objects around them strongly influence their play.

The way children combine words, objects and experiences in unconventional mixes during play is similar to how adults let their thoughts freely associate when they're dreaming. Children take from what's around them and blend them into their own memories: the whim of the moment, visual impressions, the room's furniture, unexpressed needs, bodily experiences, what Mummy just said. From all this, they create a wonderful collage to draw on: back in play, they may test all kinds of words and sounds to see if they are usable, and if the other children understand.

It can be damaging for a child to do only one activity for long periods. For example, to ask a child to walk at a monotonous adult pace during a walk is a form of over-

exertion, as is having a child sit and put beads in a frame for an hour. Children need life and movement. It isn't a sign of lack of concentration if they frequently switch from one activity to another. Children are sanguine beings: they want to fly from flower to flower like a butterfly, to see what is on offer. Then, after a while, they fly back to the first flower again.

A quick word about television and computers in relation to change and transformation. Television appears to offer variety and movement, but in fact, children watching TV sit still for too long. Their eye muscles are held in a constant position, because the distance to the TV is always the same. And there's no depth to a TV image, like there is for a mirror.

It's the same for computer games. Children can become fascinated with, even addicted to, the glitzy world of computer games and apps, from a young age these days. They can sit for hours doing puzzles or 'drawing', denying their innate desire for movement. Parents might feel that some of the games are educational, but it's still important to limit the amount of time children spend sitting still, and encourage variety in their play.

Repetition

Children need balance, so just because they like movement and change, doesn't mean they want everything to change all the time. On the contrary, repetition is important, such as hearing the same story again and again. They soon know if the words aren't the same each time; the known pattern brings delight and security. They know the story and so can 'dare' to be frightened by trolls and giants. An unknown story with an unknown ending can get too scary.

Three and four-year-olds appreciate simple funny stories and rhymes like The House That Jack Built, The Pancake That Ran Away, The Seven Little Kids, Goldilocks and the Three Bears, The Three Little Pigs, and so on. If we adults can overcome our frustration over repeating the same words, we'll notice how children absorb and enjoy the limited vocabulary. It's the words' relation to each other – the rhythm and the melody – that they grasp, and then use in their play.

A short rhyme or verse read every night becomes a secure entrance to the world of sleep. If weekdays have a certain rhythm, and weekends another, children will soon experience the rhythm of the week.

We can also appreciate more detail about something, the more often we do it. For example, if we go for a walk in a certain forest every Sunday, more and more details eventually appear – strange little creatures that we didn't see the first times, remarkable flowers, crooked branches, beautiful stones, the chirping of birds, and the rustle of mice. If we tell a story many times over, we recognise more little details than if we hear it only once and then immediately hear another.

But remember balance: freshness is important too. A little Christmas play with simple dolls can seem new every year: the child has changed during the year, so they watch the play with new, fresh eyes.

We're so anxious to show our children reality, and have them experience a wide breadth of the world. We take them sightseeing, dragging them to museums and zoos, to entertain and inform. At the zoo, we rush ahead impatiently – 'come on, or we won't have time to see the bears!' – even while the child is absorbed in watching a little ant walk across the zoo path. And when we get home, exhausted from hours of trudging round the zoo, we discover that the child's favourite thing from the day was the little ant.

Summary

Children gradually grow into their bodies, and conquer language at the same time.

Rhymes and verses are nourishment for children's imagination and language development.

Let preschool children live in the here and now.

Young children don't understand caricatures. Give them toys which capture the essence of an animal without being too realistic.

Avoid puzzles with faces or bodies split into pieces or surrounded by black lines.

Games of change and transformation are key for this age, with inspiration coming from children's outer environment.

One-sided activities overexert children. Let them alternate between activity and movement.

Repetition offers security. A repeated good-night verse will facilitate falling asleep. Hearing the same song many times makes us more sensitive to it.

When exploring the world, start at home and the local neighbourhood; only later go on longer trips. Start with the ant, not the zoo!

Dolls with simple clothes and a doll's bed

Recommendations for play and toys, ages 3–4

Children don't need much to be able to play. Give them scraps from your own activities and let them take part in your activities. Avoid colouring books where children are encouraged to fill in ready-made black outlines.

Some suggestions:

Knot doll

Large, simple doll

A few clothes for the doll that are easy to put on and take off

A doll's bed made of cardboard, a wooden cradle, doll carriage/pram, or sleeping bag

A mattress, pillow, blanket and sheet for a doll's bed (when the child can manage to make the bed)

Various pieces of cloth to sew with or to wrap a doll in

Some large cloths in cheerful colours for making houses or dressing up

A funny hat, an old purse, some pieces of jewellery

Gold paper, tissue paper, crepe paper, nontoxic glue

Block crayons, wax crayons, and large sheets of thick paper

Large wooden truck, a few smaller cars

Various small pieces of wood for building

A few simple animals

Moving toys: jumping jack, hens that peck, old men that saw

Little baskets or boxes for collecting pretty stones and other things

A rocking horse

A table which, when put on its side, can be transformed with the help of some blankets into a store, house, car, etc.

Outdoors: bucket and spade, ball, small wheelbarrow, pinwheel, bark boats, swing, etc.

5. Age Five to Six

Thoughts and concepts

Five-year-olds are, generally, quite calm and content. They can actually be quiet for quite long periods of time, and give the impression of having greater purposefulness and composure. They have matured enough to be able to find words to express their disappointments, rather than rolling on the floor kicking and screaming. They have started to 'philosophise'.

'Mum, what do you think is the best on people?' my five-year-old asked seriously. He listened to my answer, then said, 'I think the best on people is their hands – and arms.' And he had indeed drawn a person with large hands, as five-year-olds often do.

'Mum, isn't it strange that we can see something inside our head, even if it isn't here.' He had discovered inner concepts.

Another day he pondered over why long-distance ice skaters, whose legs moved so slowly, nevertheless made faster progress than ice hockey players, whose legs moved so quickly.

'Mum, where did I come from? Who made everything in

the whole world?' In this, he wasn't asking for a lecture on sexuality, theology or gas nebulae.

'Where was I when you were small?' He wants to hear that he was somewhere. The idea that 'you didn't exist' is too incomprehensible, and it hurts to hear that 'when you die, you don't exist anymore'. It's better for him to hear that 'before you came to us you were somewhere, and you looked at all the people, and you chose a mummy and daddy and came to us.' It's nice for me, as a parent, to imagine that my children chose me and nobody else, because then I must make an effort to show them they made a good choice.

When five-year-olds ask questions, we must listen intently. How much do they want to know? We strengthen their ability to form concepts if we give them pictorial descriptions that their imagination can work with. Photographs of the cosmos and childbirth, on the other hand, limit and inhibit their imagination. So if a child asks what their stomach looks like, vividly describe a large sack where all the food goes, but don't show them a TV programme or book where a human being is taken apart into organs, blood, muscles etc. That could make a child start to hurt all over, and worry that the different parts won't hold together properly. Rather, let the child's imagination take hold of the concept. Later on, once they're at school and are at a stage when they can be detatched and critical, children are mature enough to study anatomy.

An aside on reading: five-year-olds are usually very interested in letters, something which often subsides at six when they'd rather be physical and messy, but re-emerges at seven. At five, letters, like television, can fascinate a child so much that they can spend a long time sitting still with magazines and books. And although we can't prevent a child from learning to read early, letters are too abstract to be good stimulation for younger children, and spending a lot of time reading can limit a child's range of experiences. Additionally, afterwards, there is often a fatigue reaction in the form of noisy overactivity. Children should get to hear as many stories as possible, but also be given lots of opportunities for active play with other children.

Free role play

The inspiration for playing at this age starts to come from within. Children have a clearer idea about what they want to enact than previously, so the external environment isn't as influential as before. They have an inner image of the play.

Listen to some five-year-olds as they play. First they sketch a framework for the play, and then they speak in the past tense:

'Let's say you were a man who came to visit, and I was a mummy who was going out with her baby, and you had a high hat.'

When all the important facts are established, a child says, 'Now we'll begin,' and then they start talking in the present tense.

'Knock knock, says the man, knock, now I'm going in – hello, isn't the daddy home today?'

'No, he's out right now.'

'Oh dear.'

Now a pause: the actors notice that the high hat is missing. They rush to the dressing-up box and get a hat.

'This can be the hat.' Now that their play corresponds to their inner image of how it was supposed to be, they theatrically repeat the whole beginning.

Play at this age has a special mood. When they were younger, the borders between play and other activities were quite loosely defined. But now, children can suddenly stop playing. Conflicts often arise because children have different inner images of how it should be: 'No, let's play something else now,' or 'If you won't do it like I said, I'm not going to play!' They're now capable of actively withdrawing from the play when it doesn't suit them any more.

Drawing

Children's drawings can reveal many things that they can't yet express in words. If we can interpret their drawings, we can sometimes help them address something that's worrying them. But equally, if we show too obvious an interest in their picture, they can become self-conscious and no longer able to create spontaneously.

If we enthusiastically praise everything that they draw and immediately hang it on the wall, they'll soon start to produce drawings for our sake, not theirs. It's not the result that should be admired, but the activity itself. We love that they draw, and so they fill up the whole paper with happy colours. It's nice to save sample pictures every now and then, but without a big fuss.

We should restrain ourselves from always asking our children what a drawing represents, because they might feel forced to tell us things they're not really experiencing. But of course we should listen when they bring us a picture and want to tell us what it shows.

Give them just a few sheets at a time, so they don't get wasteful or sloppy.

Maria is six years old. She wants to draw, but hesitates for a long time with a crayon in her hand. 'What will I draw?' Finally she decides, 'I'll draw a horse running in a field.' She starts: the horse is brown, naturally, and the grass is green. She has become a realist. The four-year-old Maria would happily have drawn a brown sun and purple grass, but six-year-old Maria is more particular.

'There's no yellow crayon, I can't draw the sun!' Maria also observes her drawing critically, and crumples it up, dissatisfied. 'It's not very good,' she says. The picture didn't match her inner image of how a horse in a field looks.

In the same way, a whole play activity can stop if six-year-old children can't find something to be a cash register when they're playing shopping. They look for a suitable object: perhaps the toy dresser with the drawer will do. When they were four, they would have happily used any old shoe or block.

Will you play with me?

If Maria is alone, she'll often try to get one of her parents involved in her game. Many parents dread hearing the words, 'Will you play with me?' Dad is given a role, and Maria watches carefully to make sure he stays in character.

This can sometimes become tyrannical: the poor parents can't ever be themselves, and the whole house becomes inhabited by invisible friends on whom they can't sit down by mistake.

Other children tell endless stories about their own secret kingdom. These fantasies are images of what is happening inside the child. They should be respected, but not be the main focus of your time together. It's reasonable for parents to want to spend time with their real-life child, not all her invisible friends! (You should also think about whether these day-dreams might have arisen from a longing for friends, or from a feeling of not being loved.)

On the other hand, parents often think the game is going to be more demanding than it actually is. They imagine they're going to have to lay on at least half-an-hour's entertainment, and so they say no. In fact, surprisingly little is often actually demanded if the children have become used to playing by themselves. Mum can keep sewing and just stick out a foot to get bandaged, and Maria is happy playing hospitals. A rumbling growl as Dad sits reading can be enough to convince Maria that he's a wild boar.

One time, my own daughter came and sat next to me. 'Mum! Let's pretend that you're a mummy, and I'm your daughter!'. It took all my self-control not to burst out, 'But I *am* your mummy!' I made the effort, however, and soon got a glimpse of the fun possibilities of being a different mummy to a different child: I disguised my voice, pulled my glasses down to the tip of my nose, and pretended to be very strict. My daughter was delighted – it was another mother!

Dolls

A few children don't like playing with dolls. The daughter of a doll merchant, for example, might not want to have anything to do with them. And I've heard the story of a six-year-old who got a big plastic doll that could talk: it wasn't long before the doll was taken apart, the speech mechanism taken out, the doll thrown in a corner and the speech mechanism put to bed and cared for!

Most children who are given a plastic doll, however, do play with it. They fantasise and talk to the doll just like they do with their soft doll, or other toys. But, as we explored in Chapter 1, the modelled face of a plastic doll means it's often given a particular role or is confined to a narrower range within the child's play. The same is true of all toys with pronounced features: caricatured toys such as Punch are limited to being Punch: he can't sometimes be Judy (see the previous chapter for more on caricatures). A doll whose features are only suggested will give children greater freedom in their play.

Losing a doll

Losing a favourite doll can be a terrible tragedy. It's comparable to losing a close relative. The child must therefore be allowed to work through their grief and loss, and be comforted. Don't say things like, 'It was only a doll,' or 'We'll get you a new one.' We would never say that to a parent who had lost a child. But we can comfort the child with words like 'Perhaps your doll went to another home where another boy or girl is happy to have it; and maybe you'll soon find another little friend who will need you.'

For some children the doll can never be replaced, but they might be able to transfer their strong feelings to a living pet instead. Other children find a totally different doll and start to feel connected to it.

A big baby doll is an especially good toy if a child has a new baby brother or sister. It could even inherit real baby clothes (with the sleeves or legs folded up). But beware of real baby cream, which can stain a soft baby doll! Most children will be fine with pretend 'air-cream'.

You can make a simple doll's house for small dolls from a box, or on a shelf. Homemade furniture made from little boxes and pieces of wood will stimulate a child to make more. Beeswax is good for making little utensils; the child can draw little pictures for the walls; older children could weave mini rugs.

If, however, a child is given a large pre-made doll's house with lots of rooms and detail, sooner or later they'll probably move the doll out of the grand house and into a random corner with some bits of furniture. It's more challenging for children's imaginations to set up the house themselves, than playing with the ready-made house. Grand doll's houses are probably expressions of a grown-up's desire to play, but for children they usually end up as curios.

Sense impressions

The word 'impression', something literally pressed into me, conveys how we are shaped by what we see, hear, feel, smell, taste and experience. Sense impressions like these, and our ability to interpret them, make it possible for us to orient ourselves in time. It's important that we take care of our senses, therefore, and don't allow them to become dulled.

Children who live in a city are often surrounded all day by the constant sounds of the city. In any location, subtle faint sounds may be drowned out by traffic, noise in the nursery, or noise in the home such as loud music or the TV. Consequently, children may become afraid of the quiet of the night – or become loud-voiced.

The senses need time to adjust. It's better to start with simple and subtle sense impressions, and move on to complicated or strong impressions later. For example, when children start to listen to music, start with single notes, not a whole orchestra. A single flute or a few subtle tones from a string instrument work well. The best thing for children's hearing is to listen to songs sung live – not recorded – and to simple pieces from a single instrument. The ear first needs to know what is quiet, in order to handle the whole range of sounds.

Children are influenced – impressed upon – in other ways too. Sometimes young children take on the physical traits of the much-loved adults around them: there are recorded examples of children who start to walk with a limp, even though their legs are healthy, just because one of their parents walks with a limp.

Much-loved toys can influence physical traits too. Falling asleep with a floppy, soulless doll will not instill a firm, straight posture in a child, whereas a healthy-looking doll with a firm, warm body will help give a child stability.

Summary

Five and six-year-olds are, at least sometimes, calm and 'philosophical'.

When they ask questions about the world, it's best to give answers which leave room for their imaginations to thrive.

Children at this age draw more inspiration for their play from inside.

Children often need less parental participation than expected to get started with their play.

A doll with suggested features, and a simple doll's house, are best for children's imaginations, and can change endlessly.

Sense impressions are literally 'pressed in' to children, shaping them from a young age.
Be careful what impressions your child receives.

The senses need time to mature. Start with simple and subtle experiences of colour, music, dance, and so on.

Yarn dolls can inhabit a miniature world

Recommendations for play and toys, ages 5–6

When a child has accumulated too many toys, don't forget to take some away.

Some suggestions:

A knot doll, made by the child

A dress-up doll with clothes; a baby doll with nappies (diapers) and cradle

A whole family of doll's house dolls or yarn dolls

A simple doll's house in a box or on a shelf

Homemade doll furniture and utensils

Beeswax. You can buy it in cakes; it smells good, comes in good colours, and is nontoxic. Warm it in the hands and shape it: as soon as it hardens, it can be played with. Can be re-used forever

Pieces of fabric, needle and thread in a little sewing kit

Pieces of fabric for playing and dressing-up clothes in a bag or suitcase

Wax crayons, watercolours, broad paint brushes, large sheets of paper

Coloured paper to cut; nontoxic glue

Wooden scraps, wooden wheels, sticks, hammer and nails (help with sawing!), sandpaper, file, and wood glue

Blue clay

Cars

Soft and hard animals; fence blocks for barn

Empty boxes and jars

Baskets for little things

Swing

Movable picture of favourite story

Outdoors: bucket and spade, ball, cart to pull, wagon, skipping (jump) rope, marbles, high swing, tops, kites, boats, paper swallows

6. Age Seven and Up: Schoolchildren

Transformation and imagination

Children who are ready for school undergo a remarkable transformation. They somehow stand taller, and look us in the eye in a different way. Almost every cell of their body has been changed, and the change of teeth has begun: these children have made their own bodies in which to continue growing.

A new seven-year period starts here, which will conclude with puberty. In this period, memory, imagination and feeling are especially dominant. Children are curious about life outside home or preschool. They want to test their powers, and find new authorities. Their imagination flourishes, and they welcome images and archetypes from fairy tales, fables, legends and myths.

Never again are we in such perfect control of bodily movement as we are in this second seven-year period. Just watch a school child sliding down a slide, then standing up and climbing back up with perfect balance. Their body is an instrument they have learnt to play like expert musicians, producing rare and beautiful tones.

This is also the 'quick-to-learn' age; children devour

information, gathering data and absorbing material for their memories. Many school-age children develop special interests and soon know everything worth knowing about seashells, train schedules, or endangered animals. They're collectors too: some might collect stamps, labels or tickets; others have secret codes and languages.

This in-depth knowledge is used by children in their fantasy worlds, in building models, making drawings or inventing miniature societies. School-age children want to collect, organise and summarise.

Later, during puberty, many of these skills are lost for a period during which teenagers can be unhappy with themselves, and with everyone else. They become critical, analysing everything from a distance. Their experience of their body gets in the way: they can't think of anything except themselves, and the world situation. They don't study with the same kind of concentration as in the second seven-year period.

Play: the group and rules

When children start school, they compare themselves to other children. They often try to fit into the group, doing what others do. At playtime (recess), for example, the group can be strict about the rules of the game being played: if someone is late, they might not get to play at all.

Only the bravest children can disregard the group and the group's decision. Anyone who's even a little shy won't dare insist that they're allowed to play. Adults or older children can help, once in a while, by organising games where everyone joins in.

When children discover that they can make up their own rules for a particular ball game, or hopscotch, or chase game, they soon will, and with great variation. Children can end up fighting seriously over whether a particular action is permitted. Before you know it, they start making rules for everything: which door you have to use on the bus; how you have to walk along that bit of pavement (sidewalk), balancing on the edge; how many marbles you have to stake in the marble game; how you have to say a certain chant when you skip rope. Some children carry trading cards or other swappable items which are won or traded according to strict market rules. Having learned that people abide by rules in order to live with each other, schoolchildren regularly practise social dynamics in their play.

Drawing

Children of school age have different drawing skills and attitudes than in the first seven-year period. Their drawings often lose some of the power and boldness that they previously had, and children are more likely to check to see what their neighbour is drawing, and adapt their drawing to certain norms: this is good, this is bad. They might make an effort to draw as well as an older, admired friend. At this age, they need a lot of encouragement to draw and paint spontaneously.

A seven-year-old boy, let's call him Jack, saw a lovely view and exclaimed, 'Oh look, how beautiful!' Previously he only saw that the clouds moved across the sky, or that a car moved in the distance. But now he is starting to enjoy the beauty in what he sees – which in turn makes him more critical of his own creations.

As Jack gets a bit older, he becomes more ambitious: he tries to use perspective in his drawings. He can also draw a face, and a whole person, quite well. He has learnt what a face looks like, and consequently he can play with his knowledge in drawing caricatures and comic figures.

By the age of nine, Jack has reached the level of linguistic and mental development that means he can understand adults' jokes. He starts to draw his own comic strips and magazines.

Dolls

Many children who might not previously have played much with dolls now enter a real doll-playing phase. They take their doll with them everywhere, they want things for the doll, they put the doll to bed every night before they go to bed; they make clothes and tiny belongings for the doll.

There are a multitude of dead-eyed, stiff plastic dolls like Barbie and Action Man available in stores, either skinny with impossibly long legs, or with ridiculously overgrown muscles. They have thousands of accessories, from horses and swimming pools to racing cars and other status symbols. Do we want to covey the values and materialistic lifestyle inherent in these types of dolls to our children? As an alternative, try making a small dress-up doll for a child. If the doll's hair is made of strong cotton thread, it can be combed and styled well, and school-age children can themselves make clothes for the dainty doll. In fact, even children who consider themselves too old to play with dolls will still enjoy making doll's clothes, and quietly inventing a little adventure for the doll as they do so.

From about ten years and up, children can start to make dolls for themselves. The large dress-up dolls are the most difficult, especially getting the proportions right and assembling them. But children will keep asking for help, or equally tell you that they've decided not to bind off the head (too much work) or that it really doesn't need feet, does it? Cute mini-dolls to slip into a pocket can be made by simply reducing the size of the patterns in proportion.

Saying goodbye

When the time comes to say goodbye to a doll, let the child take the lead. Don't say things like, 'You're so big, why do you drag that dirty old doll around all the time?' Instead, let the child realise themselves that they've left their childhood behind. If we force them to throw away a beloved old doll, they might lose their trust in us. As long as the doll has a little bit of their soul in it, they can't separate without some pain. But one day, the child will notice that the doll is empty – the butterfly has left its pupa – and they'll suggest that we give it away, or put it away.

Finding a purpose

In other cultures, seven-year-olds may already be incorp-orated into adult life and have been given duties, according to ability, to help support their family. In the developed

A dress-up doll for a school-age child. They can also be made smaller than shown here.

world, children of this age are largely spared this burden; there is, thankfully, no longer child labour, which can steal an entire childhood.

On the other hand, children need meaningful, purposeful activities just like adults. Children shouldn't be entirely relegated from adults' 'important' tasks. It's not easy, though, in our appliance-rich homes to find useful things for children to do, even school-age children. A lot of practical chores are either deemed too dangerous, or have been transformed into complex mechanical activities; compare, for example, the process of using a washing machine to washing clothes by hand.

So how are our children going to learn useful skills which help them grow into our society? How will they gain a feeling of responsibility for getting food, and a roof over their heads? It's important that we do find suitable household tasks for them. They can help to wash fine woollen clothes by hand; they can mix dough, whip cream, and cut vegetables (with age-appropriate knives). They might be able to buy one or two things from the corner grocery store. They can even cook food, with good instructions – and mistakes don't matter.

Some children are realists, and will happily busy themselves with practical tasks, doing what's needed with an air of importance. Others are imaginative bohemians, who only do what they want to do. Most children, though, are sensitive to being forced to do something. They don't understand the democratic reasoning which says that everyone in the family must make their own bed, and do the dishes once a week. But as we've seen, a three-year-old enjoys helping to do the dishes when Mum's doing them –

and out of that joy and habit, the three-year-old can become a very helpful eight-year-old.

Purposeful toys

A category of toy which often disappoints children are those which are made to look like realistic, purposeful items, but which in fact aren't fit for real purpose. This category includes toy tools, toy instruments, toy pots and pans, toy binoculars, and so on. When the child tries to use the toy saw in a meaningful way, it bends and isn't sharp. And the doll saucepan smells of burnt paint when it's put on the stove.

It's much more fun to be given real tools, real saucepans, real instruments – not as many as adults have, because then there's nothing left to wish for, but durable items which work. A little box with a needle, thread and scissors, for example, and a few nice pieces of fabric, are lovely for sewing some simple doll's clothes. A simple recorder or harmonica on which to pick out some notes is also a good choice.

Toy guns

A nine-year-old boy, Harry, nagged his mum for a long time to get him a toy gun. He even woke up in the middle of night and called out that he wanted a gun. His mother gave in, and bought him a big toy revolver. Well, what harm could it do? Boys will be boys, and boys love playing games of war and shooting, right? Harry took his toy revolver to school and proceeded to run around the playground, pretend-shooting other children. The gun even made a loud 'bang' noise. All the other children stopped their games and looked at him. Some younger ones were frightened and started crying. His mother was mortified.

In our heightened times, with security issues uppermost in people's minds, I would suggest it's even less appropriate now to give children toy guns or weapons. I don't believe that children naturally need to play war games, if they've grown up in peacetime. The only reason for this kind of play is for children who have lived through a war, and need to 'play war' to help work through their terrible experiences.

Children do need excitement and tension – to sneak up on each other, crawl around in the bushes in the dark, or explore a creepy, squeaky attic. But it's important to teach children never to aim anything which looks like a gun at another human being.

Children who see violence on television or the internet may need ways to work through these sense impressions. Indeed, even if they only watch peaceful TV programmes, their passive staring for a long period of time can lead to pent-up energy, which may be released in uncontrolled or aggressive behaviour. If you feel your child needs to work through a particular sense impression, they could pretend-shoot at a target board, or pretend-shoot a rabbit for tea – but never pretend-shoot another person.

The rhythm of the year

Children want to feel longing and anticipation. Holidays throughout the year offer fine opportunities for making the home a little extra exciting and festive. For parents who don't find meaning in Christmas or Easter, there are other annual opportunities, such as birthdays.

Birthdays are very important to children, and birthday children should be somehow honoured. They could have a special chair to sit on (an armchair could be called a 'celebration chair' and dragged into the kitchen), or a beautiful wreath could be placed on their head (if it's wintertime, you could make a wreath from tissue paper or felt). The birthday child gets waited on by everyone else, and gets to choose their favourite meal for dinner. Birthday songs can be sung and played. Everyone enjoys the birthday, not just the birthday child.

Other celebration opportunities might include a day trip out every autumn or spring to a certain place with friends, grilling food over a fire and sleeping in sleeping bags.

Christmas is usually the most fun time for children, particularly the advent period leading up to the big day. Presents and decorations are made, and there's baking, rustling and bustling. The house is decorated and seen with new eyes.

It's a good way for children to experience that another year has gone by for them. Last year, they couldn't move the rolled-out gingerbread cookies onto the baking sheet, but this year they can. Last year they couldn't reach the craft table, but this year they can.

The joy of preparing surprises, and of hoping for some yourself, is wonderful. Many school-age children can keep busy for hours making Christmas presents: beeswax is a wonderful material to work with at this time of year and makes lovely things, such as attaching beeswax figures to white candles. It doesn't take too long, either, so children don't tire of it. Pictures for the window are another good craft activity: glue tissue paper onto waxed paper, and make a smart frame from solid white paper.

Apart from festivals and birthdays, the change of the seasons is a solid base for most preschool and kindergarten-age activities. There are songs suitable for spring, summer, autumn and winter. During harvest time, children can grind grain and bake bread. In winter, they can dip candles; in spring, make little birdhouses. Activities like these especially help city-bound children to engage with the seasons and the natural world.

Summary

School-age children welcome images which fuel their feeling and imagination.

They play games with complex rules, which require cooperation.

Now that they know what a face looks like, they can start to draw caricatures.

Parents should try to find soft, non-commercial alternatives to Barbie and Action Man.

Children should be given simple, meaningful tasks to make them feel part of family life.

Give children real tools and pans when they want to make things or cook, and real instruments when they want to play music.

Toy guns are dangerous. You can rob a bank with a replica gun.

Annual festivals and the change of the seasons offer many exciting activities for children and parents.

A doll's house with small dolls and wooden furniture

Recommendations for play and toys, ages seven and up

A few suggestions:

A small soft doll, with clothes

Needle, thread and fabric for sewing

Expanded collection of dress-up clothes, veils, hats, belts

Make-up: wax crayons are good if the child's face is first rubbed with grease

Doll's house dolls, knot or yarn dolls

Doll's house furniture and accessories

Beeswax for a multitude of craft projects

Wax crayons, watercolour paints, smaller paintbrushes, coloured pencils

Pieces of wood, wooden wheels, a few real tools with a safe storage place and close instruction in how to care for and sharpen them

Pieces of fur, leather, textile glue

String

Blue clay, plaster

Soft and hard animal toys

Weaving loom, knitting needles, crochet hook, yarns

Empty boxes – for example, for making a puppet theatre

Board games such as Ludo (Parcheesi), dominoes, Chinese checkers, Mouse Trap

Outdoors: kites, tree houses, homemade pedal car, high swing, their own garden plot, toy boat, toy airplane

A few final thoughts for this age:

School children can make their own jigsaw puzzles: paint a picture on plywood, then using watercolours, sketch the outline of the pieces; varnish; saw out pieces with a fretsaw

Wait until the children can sit still for long periods and pick through the small parts before you give them detailed model construction sets.

Watch out for toxic glue!

A larger-scale construction set such as Meccano is a wonderful but expensive present for a nine or ten-year-old.

By nine or ten, a child can work with pewter or plaster, or form items in clay and have them fired

7. Further Thoughts on Creative Play

In the adult world, we work because other people need the objects we make and the services we offer. The impulse for our work comes from external sources.

Creative play is children's equivalent of work, but only in the sense that it is an important and serious activity. With children, the impulse comes from within; play is for them, not for someone else. When a child is presented with a ready-made toy, and told, 'Go and play with this!' it's like an external order. The source of play needs to be the children themselves.

Learning through living

Sophie's parents are worried that she hasn't yet learned to button buttons. So they hurry out and buy her a toy: two pieces of fabric which can be buttoned together. The purpose of the toy is simply to button buttons. Sophie realises on her third attempt that it has no other meaning or reason.

In the real world, we button buttons for very good reasons. We button up cardigans or sweaters to stay warm, and we button up jeans to stop them falling down. That's why it's much more fun for Sophie to button up all of her mother's coat buttons when she isn't looking – it's funny when she tries to put the coat on! – or to help her little brother button his jacket.

Sophie's parents also want to teach her the difference between flour, sugar and salt. They make up three identical jars containing the three substances. 'Let's taste them, Sophie. Do they taste different? This one is salt, this is sugar, and this is flour.' Then the phone rings, and Sophie is left alone for a moment. When they return, her parents find her kneading a sticky mess on the kitchen table: Sophie has mixed the contents of the jars with water, and is having a lovely time 'baking'. 'Oh no,' they say, 'now we can't tell which one is which any more!' They've entirely missed the point that Sophie has made her own wonderful pie.

The moral of the story is: let children learn by living, and don't stop them from living by trying to teach them.

For preschool children, it's the everyday household activities which are the most fun. Getting your own piece of bread dough and making rolls is much better than making pretend rolls from blue-coloured salty play dough which you can't bake or eat, and which is then thrown away.

A hiding place

The purpose of a hiding place for children is that they can go there and truly hide. It's no fun hiding in a place when everyone knows where you are. Children want to go somewhere where they can pretend that they're lost, parentless and miserable; if everyone knows where you are, they're not going to cry when they discover you missing, are they?

Sophie has hidden herself in a secret place in the attic. She sits there and imagines what it would be like to run away, managing on your own, maybe hidden in the cargo hold of a big ocean-going liner. She is in the security of her home, but imagines she has disappeared without a trace.

In doing so, children are trying to understand their role within the family, who they are and how others view them. Give them the space to do it.

Replica toys

Go into a toy store and look at the whole range of merchandise. How many of the toys could actually be used for free, creative play?

Replica toys, such as toy cars which are made to look exactly like the life-size version, are a particular problem. Children are given miniatures of things from the adult world, as if children were just mini-adults, impatient to grow up.

Fortunately, most children can rise above these kinds of toys – in their play they can transform a Mini Cooper into a Chevy, or perhaps a meatball. The purpose of play is for children to develop, exercise their senses, and grow into versatile individuals – not to lust after adult status symbols.

Sophie has been given a 'real' child-sized vacuum cleaner made of plastic. It can vacuum, and has little paper bags to collect the dust. But we have to ask: do toy manufacturers, or the person who gave the gift, think that Sophie will over-tax her imagination if she has to *pretend* that her vacuum cleaner vacuums up dust? Does Sophie play at vacuuming because she thinks the room is dirty? No! She does it because she wants to imitate the activities of the adults around her. She doesn't need a toy that actually vacuums. (If sometime she does want to clean up, she can use a brush or the home's real vacuum cleaner, and be pleased at the result.)

The artist

Imagine an artist who's working on a painting. He has a vision for what he wants to create, and makes sketches. A friend comes over and stands watching for a minute. Then the friend rushes out and returns half an hour later, with an oil painting of a similar scene to the one the artist is creating.

'Look what I got for you! You can have it, so you won't have to work as hard on your painting any more.' The good friend waits for thanks and gratitude. The artist picks up the painting, puts his foot right through it, and throws it to one side. He says nothing to his former friend.

Alternatively, if the artist is more insecure, perhaps he slumps his shoulders, then starts tearing up his own sketches, throwing them in the wastebasket and wondering why he ever became an artist in the first place.

Now imagine the artist is a child, who's just been given a plastic telephone when he was immersed in playing with a shoe, as the receiver, and a string, as the cord.

We must meet children's striving to create with respect.

The collector

One time, I was in a toy store looking for large white paper sheets (which they didn't have). A grandmother came in to buy something for her grandson who would soon be turning six. The grandmother checked the whole wall of toy cars; she was clearly familiar with the different makes and models. She turned to the salesperson.

'Don't you have any more models?' she asked, disappointed.

'This is everything,' said the salesperson. 'Is there really nothing suitable?'

'Don't you have that new ambulance that was due out, the one with the real siren sound?'

'I'm sorry, it hasn't arrived yet, but there are lots of other ambulances here. Let's see, here's a nice one, with a real stretcher.'

The grandmother looked thoughtfully at the ambulance. 'No, you see, my grandson already has that one, and all the other models here. He wants something new!'

The salesperson and I stared, speechless, at the grandmother. I started to mumble something about maybe giving the boy a plain wooden car which could endlessly becomes all kinds of new models. But she didn't hear me, and left the shop.

Although older children can become collectors, this preschool boy had clearly come to it too young. He was a victim of consumer thinking, and had been transformed into a collector, instead of being an artist. His room had turned into a museum instead of being a studio.

But it's what they want

Another day I was in a different toy store. I told the salesman that I wanted a toy bus, a simple thing made of wood. The salesman frowned then eagerly showed me his best bus model toys.

'This one's a Volvo, look how real it is. Volvo themselves have approved it.'

'But I just want a simple bus – a long piece of wood with wheels under it, something that shows the characteristics of a bus but not much detail.'

He looked at me distastefully. 'But, my dear, we couldn't sell something like that. It has to be the real thing! Children want real model cars. It's what they want!'

I thanked him and left. But it's what they want ... Do children actually want everything they say they want? Children don't always know what's best for them – that's one reason they have parents. Children can have a raging fever and still want to go outside on their bicycle.

Tired parents are often quick to give in. 'He really wants that car, let him have it [and there won't be a fuss].' But deep down, their child is disappointed at their lack of involvement. He gets the car, and then gets bored, so he wants another.

It's not cruel for parents to say, 'No, you can't have that car,' as long as they add, 'but when we get home we'll do something fun together.'

Children as consumers

Most of the time, especially with preschool children, children don't have money. When they want a toy, an adult buys it for them. But occasionally, perhaps after a birthday, a child has some money to spend. Then, the child becomes a consumer.

Olivia is five years old. Her father takes her to a toy store to spend her Christmas money from her grandmother. There are so many different things she could buy. She wants so many different things. She has to choose – but she can't!

'Do you want the boat or the train?' ask her father patiently.

'Both.'

'You can only have one thing sweetheart.'

'Umm, umm, the boat.'

Finally, a decision. But it's not really a choice, it's just a guess. Olivia is only guessing that she wants the boat.

Back at home, Olivia says to her mother, 'Umm, maybe next I can get the train...?' And her mother thinks she is ungrateful.

The fact is, children live so powerfully in the present that they are not able to anticipate their feelings in the future – not even an hour ahead. If you really want to develop your child's ability to make a choice, pick a situation where nothing is given up entirely because of the choice made. 'Which sandwich are you going to eat first, the cheese or the salami?' Olivia still gets to eat both sandwiches.

In the case of toy purchases, where only one alternative is possible, it seems more reasonable for the adult, with their knowledge of the child, to choose on the child's behalf. Olivia will, in time, learn to save money for a certain desired thing, and then the choice can be hers.

Educational toys

Many toys today are lauded or marketed as 'educational', but educational toys are simply those which train a particular skill in a child.

Jasmine is three and a half. She has been given an educational toy, a board with different sized holes in it, and a number of cylinders of corresponding thickness, to be fitted into the holes. Jasmine dutifully inserts the cylinders. The idea is that after a few tries, or maybe a few days, she'll be able to put all the right cylinders in the right holes. She will have a new skill. But once she's done it, what then? The toy is finished with, of no further interest. You could say, it doesn't hurt for Jasmine to have a few different toys like this. Well no, it might not hurt, but by giving children educational toys we are arbitrarily selecting particular skills

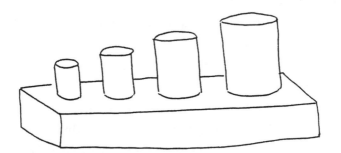

for them to learn. It's much better to let children learn from the tasks that life naturally offers.

Jasmine can practise all kinds of tricky little tasks, such as putting cubes of different sizes into corresponding holes, building a pyramid out of ever smaller pieces, discerning a certain colour or shape among others, or matching weights into pairs. But she can also practise balancing by walking along a board, hitting the mark by throwing a ball into a can, or scraping out a bowl of cookie dough so that the spoon catches all the pieces of dough in the bowl. These latter tasks are ones she chooses to do when she feels like it, when she's ready for them, and in her own way. The former 'educational' tasks are artificially determined by ready-made materials.

There is a risk, as well, that children can be trained in a one-sided way, which can lead to them losing their natural versatility, and can affect their imagination and emotional development. I don't believe that Jasmine needs an educational toy to learn to estimate the sizes of holes and cylinders. She can put the lid on a lipstick or a chapstick, she can put a pencil into a bottle, or an empty baking powder tub into an empty cocoa tub. She can try the baby food lid on a jam jar; she can put all the saucepans inside one another according to size, and put all the saucepan lids in a row. In any case, she's been putting her little hand inside every hole, thereby practising judging distance and size, ever since she was a baby.

Perhaps Jasmine was just getting immersed in a balancing act in the garden, or finding out whether the big pillow falls from the top bunk bed faster than the light little feather, when we come in and present her with an exciting wrapped package. She'll certainly stop what she's doing and set about the 'educational' task of the jigsaw puzzle, or whatever it is, because children at this age live in the present and are easily distracted. The adults will be proud when she finishes the puzzle, because finished puzzles are satisfying for adults – a result that we can see – whereas a pillow and a feather on the floor are just messy.

Another example of the different perspective that adults can have is a constant teetering on the chair at supper time, which we call 'bad manners' although it's a great way of training balance. Another might be a constant creeping around on the floor, or tiptoeing around – 'don't you have anything else to do?' – which is actually an 'investigation of how long I am when I lie down' or 'balance training on tiptoes'.

iPads and Tablets

A brief final word on iPads and other tablets, which are increasingly available to young children (and see also p.58). Introducing young children to these devices is yet another way that adult values are mistakenly projected onto children. The imagery and ease of use of tablets make them attractive but children are better served by exploring their physical environment with all their senses. That way, parents will have given children the best grounding for being able to handle digital media in a mature, competent and creative way as a teenager.

Summary

Play is children's equivalent of work. But it's work that children carry out for themselves and for their own development.

When children pretend to cook, they don't need a realistic miniature stove, which will only hinder their imagination. A box will do fine.

Children are like artists, and their play shapes their experience of life. We must not force ready-made toys onto children, but rather respect their creativity.

Some children have been transformed from creators into collectors.

Don't assume that children always know what's best for them.

Avoid situations where children must definitively choose between one thing or another. If the situation arises, make the choice on behalf of the child.

Let children play freely, developing skills which naturally arise as part of life, and which they choose for themselves. Don't direct them into intellectual problem-solving which requires them to sit still.

8. When Play Doesn't Come Naturally

I'm bored: a weakening of the will

It's Sunday, and the whole family is at home. Conrad is six years old, but he won't play. He appears to be unmotivated to do anything; he just lies on his bed facing the wall, sucking his thumb and occasionally making noises.

What are his parents' options, to help him?

1. They could nag: 'Don't just lie there! Do something!'

2. They could sit down next to him, and stroke him. They could ask questions about why he's not feeling okay: 'What's wrong? Did something happen in school last week? Do you need something? Have I said something wrong? Are you mad at Daddy? Is your brother annoying you? Do you feel ill? Tell me what's the matter, don't just shout at me! Answer! What's wrong with you? Let me help you!'

3. They could rush into Conrad's room, take out his building set and cheerfully start building: 'Come and help me make this truck! It's going to be great.'

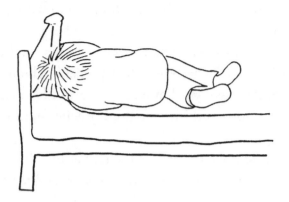

4. They could discuss Conrad's issues in another room. Does he watch too much television (which could make him passive)? Does he see adults performing chores and tasks wholeheartedly? Is he allowed to take part in our tasks? Does he participate in our lives at all? Does he know where Daddy or Mummy works, and doing what? Does he know our neighbours? Does he have material for creative play? Maybe he has too many things?

5. They could start an interesting task, such as fixing a broken window lock. They could express how difficult it is, and how much easier it would be with a certain tool – a pair of pliers, which Conrad has.

Let's examine these options so far. The first one will not be successful: nagging seldom brings results.

Option two is nice: sitting with Conrad and stroking him will make him feel that they care about him and understand him. But they don't have to say anything; if they sit quietly, there's a chance Conrad will start talking about his problems by himself. If they shower him with questions, he'll only get confused. Everything sounds equally plausible in his ears, and the more he thinks about his condition, the more worried he'll become. He'll probably choose several of the suggestions: 'Yes, I'm mad at you and Daddy, and my brother is stupid, and I have a tummy ache, and I don't like school.'

But maybe none of these is the reason for his bad mood. Young children shouldn't have to analyse their life situations: they should live spontaneously and unselfconsciously, or they might become affected and manipulative.

Option three has some good things about it: because it's a positive action, playing with children can be more effective than words. However, it must come from an honest impulse to play; if his parents are having to make an effort, Conrad will probably sense their duplicity.

Generally, if we frequently crawl around on the floor and honk and buzz, there's a risk we could be considered a clown, or something to climb on. Children can become dependent on adult assistance to be able to play; or, they can start to excitedly jump and cling on, pinching and tickling, testing the limits of adult patience. And they do this with a certain inner discomfort, because children want to be able to admire their parents.

Options four and five could be combined, and in my opinion, these are the best alternatives. Every day, his parents could look back on the day gone by and think about how Conrad was: how did he look, how did he move, how did he sound? They don't need to find reasons why things went wrong; they could just imagine him standing in front of them, focusing on him without analysing. The same approach can work with anyone we have contact with, and can help us to discover something in our way of being that we can change. Perhaps Conrad's parents are themselves bored, in which case it's less surprising that Conrad is bored too.

Perhaps other reasons will come to light: has Conrad watched so much TV, he's forgotten how to play? Is he too used to being entertained? If so, I recommend no TV watching until the age of 12. Maybe Conrad has so many toys, he's literally drowning in the mess of his room? Maybe he turns his back to escape the mess. His parents could suggest, 'Shall we help you clean up and sort out the things you've outgrown, and those that are broken? We can put those in a box in the attic.'

Perhaps Conrad feels lonely in his room. His parents could bring the ironing board in there and do ironing, or carry in an easy chair and sit next to him to read or sew. It's always more fun doing things near other people. Conrad has always made an effort to drag his toys along to the room where his parents are working, to be near them; perhaps they could show the same affection in reverse.

Six-year-olds often can't resist responding when their mother or father appears clumsy or ignorant, and they love to show how things should be done. If Conrad could assist his parents with a pair of pliers to help mend the window lock, he probably would. And before he withdraws again, they could suggest something else which needs fixing or arranging. Perhaps the furniture in Conrad's room could be rearranged, or they could get something from the attic. Then Conrad will get going, and feel revived.

It's not easy; many children today suffer from a weakening of the will. They are tired and unenterprising, they can't think of things to do, and they require constant entertainment. They need to exercise the will, by finishing what they've started, and their environment needs to inspire them to take their own initiative. Such children should never be told 'no' when they've thought of something they want to do. But in our dangerous and un-child-friendly world, there are 'no's everywhere. Ideally they need an outdoor wooded slope to go and play in freedom. They need happy song times, to see craftspeople at work, to have their own little tasks, and to have a cosy, happy home. The will can be developed, just like thinking and feeling, and activities like this can help develop it.

Too much reality

Meet Nicky. He's seven, and he's extremely imaginative – or so the adults say, as they nervously watch him whirl towards them, hair on end, hands everywhere, shaking with excitement and talking incessantly: 'And then we flew away on a moon rocket and then it crashed like THIS and everything went CRASH, BOOM, but we came down anyway, and ... oh, what a great dagger, WOW, snap like THIS, swish! That's cool – oh, boy, it got stuck in the chair! What a cool knife! And now I'd like to have the world's fastest racing car and just go flying into the finish – oh, Mum, I'm so hungry, I want a sandwich, aren't we going to eat soon? And you know what, Mum, yesterday there was a boy who kicked me right here ...'

Nicky can't play. He's not creating anything original with his thoughts – he's actually not very imaginative. He seems to receive too many sense impressions. He's insecure and unsure of himself, and he uses violence to prove himself. He's very susceptible to violence, some of which comes from TV or computer games.

Sense impressions dance a witches' dance in his head. He doesn't know what to do with them. The only way he can deal with these phantoms, and defend himself against them, is to express them in words, which helps objectify them. He wants his mother to hear all the terrible things he says, because he wants her to know what's going on inside him. He's not trying to frighten her; on the contrary, he wants her to take the phantoms away and give him warmth and love (food) instead.

Just like all children, Nicky wants the world to be good. If the opposite is shown to be the case time and again, his inner balance is disturbed and his will to live is damaged. When he's young, he should be spared seeing terrible things in newspapers and on the television. As he grows older, we'll see his will strengthen and help him to want to change the world for the better; he'll have energy left over to feel sympathy and develop understanding.

But for now, if Nicky is to live in harmony with himself and have a rich imagination, the adults around him can't talk to him as they would to an adult. He can't be expected to take any responsibility for the world; adults must keep those serious burdens to themselves for now. He must be protected from the wider world, otherwise, it'll be no fun to play.

As an aside, I don't believe that children should be completed shielded from any reality which is negative. When sad things happen to us personally, children have a right to know a bit about them, because they are realities for us which we must live with.

Fairy tales and inner reality

Fairy tales contain many fine examples of fighting the evil within ourselves, and how our good sides can triumph. If adults take the stories seriously, children will get much joy from hearing, again and again, how good beats evil. They can listen without fear to the most horrifying stories of wolves eating children and trolls turning princes to stone. Children instinctively sense that the story isn't about real wolves, but our own voracious instincts, the predator beasts within each of us.

If, however, the person reading the story doesn't see the deeper symbolism, and thinks the troll is just a fictitious character, and the castle royalist propaganda, the value of the tale for the child won't be as great. The child might have nightmares about the fairy tales, just as it does about other dangerous and inexplicable things. But when the person telling the story is open to the ancient wisdom and knowledge about human souls contained therein, the story can have a profoundly positive influence, for nearly all fairy tales have a happy ending. It will show that in all difficult inner struggles, good will win out.

Many times I've heard people say that we shouldn't read such romanticised stories to modern-day children, because they don't reflect the world they live in. In fact, I think that most children live in a little house in their inner landscape. You can see it in their drawings: even children raised in apartments live in cabins within themselves. The house symbolises the child's own body. Not until they get older do they move out, into the wider reality, and only then will they draw all kinds of houses.

Fairy tales also take place in the human interior. We all have a wicked stepmother within us who selfishly looks in the mirror; we all have trolls and dragons and dark forces which lurk in the corners of our beings and try to overpower the prince, our ego. Sometimes we calculate coldly, and then the ice monster comes with his entourage to envelop the landscape of our soul with snow. If we feel warmth of heart, and sacrifice ourselves for others, we gain entry to the orchard laden with fruit, and the prince and princess are reunited. Two sides of our personality are united in harmony.

As we saw in the story of Nicky, too much realism isn't good for children. Children shouldn't watch TV programmes about war and violence – for most children, that's not their immediate experience. Television often bears no relation to a child's life, touching neither on their home

Stretching out tentacles ... a three-year-old's drawing

environment nor on their unique personal relationships. Even with books, giving children aged three to seven realistic stories – Anya lives in an apartment, her parents often fight, this is what it's like to be in hospital, or in Antarctica – is unhelpful because such general stories have no connection with the child's own first-hand experiences. If we want to share with children the workings of human inner reality, we do so best through fairy tales and little stories of our own, and by listening to children's questions. Children can take the imagery from fairy tales, carry it and grow with it. It can help children struggle with their own difficulties: they can stretch out their feelers in the positive atmosphere of a fairy tale. But if they encounter pessimism and misery again and again, they'll pull in their tentacles, close up and suck their thumb.

Let's revisit Nicky's story. How can we help him? Try to interest him in doing practical things with his hands: scrubbing, washing windows, baking, kneading clay, sawing and nailing, painting furniture, painting pictures.

We can let him know that we understand his fears, in a roundabout way. We can tell stories about boys who go out into the fearful world and meet dragons and other terrifying things, and how they finally get the princess. Nicky won't feel overpowered by imagery from fairy tales, the way he does from images on TV. In the tales, he can protect himself from the images, because he only makes the dragon as scary as his inner vision can handle.

Summary

For children like Conrad: quietly analyse their situation. Don't shower them with questions or ask them to analyse themselves. Let them sense our love and involvement.

For under sevens, speak with actions instead of words. Awaken their interest by getting them busy with something challenging.

Let their will strengthen and develop.

For children like Nicky: they have received too many sense impressions and are overcome by phantoms which whirl around in their memory.

Clean up their experiences: decrease television (ideally to none at all); give them inner images to replace unhelpful outer ones: from fairy tales, from your own stories, from living time shared with other children and adults. Aim for a calm daily routine.

Try to anchor their lives to the here and now. Let them experience things for themselves, rather than receiving filmed or published second-hand experiences. Let them help with as many practical home tasks as possible. Let them work with their hands.

Further Reading

Crossley, Diana, *Muddles, Puddles and Sunshine*, Hawthorn Press

Dancy, Rahima Baldwin, *You Are Your Child's First Teacher*, Celestial Arts

Jaffke, Freya, *Celebrating Festivals with Children*, Floris Books
—, *On the Play of the Child*, Waldorf Early Childhood Association of North America
—, *Toymaking with Children*, Floris Books
—, *Work and Play in Early Childhood*, Floris Books

Jenkinson, Sally, *The Genius of Play*, Hawthorn Press

Neuschütz, Karin, *Creative Wool*, Floris Books
—, *Making Soft Toys*, Floris Books
—, *Sewing Dolls*, Floris Books

Oldfield, Lynne, *Free to Learn*, Hawthorn Press

Opie, Iona and Peter, *Children's Games in Street and Playground*, Floris Books

Index